PLUROTUS FLORIDA

(THE DELICIOUS OYSTER MUSHROOM)

RAHUL KUMAR

To the farmers of India who work relentlessly to feed all of us.

Contents

Preface

Proteins are the essential components of protoplasm, forming the physical basis of life. Proteins are very important for growth and repair of the body and are of prime biological importance. Their acute deficiency in the food causes retardation of the physical and mental growth. Deficiency of proteins causes PEM (Protein Energy Malnutrition) diseases in infants like marasmus and kwashiorkar. Mushrooms are rich in protein and constitute a valuable source of supplementary food. Use of mushrooms can contribute positively in facing the challenge of world-wide food shortage, originating with rapidly expanding human population. *Pleurotus florida* (an Oyster mushroom locally known as the Dhingri mushroom in India) is an edible mushroom having excellent flavour and taste.

Present handbook deals with the nutritional value of edible mushrooms as a non-conventional source of proteins with special reference to the common edible Oyster mushrooms. *Pleurotus florida* is one of the most popular agriculturally important Oyster mushrooms. Present book deals with the cultivation of this mushroom right from the development of inoculum to the harvesting of the final fruiting bodies by standard protocol. This handbook may prove beneficial to the farmers and those who are interested in mushroom culture. This handbook may also be used as a manual of Oyster mushroom farming.

Rahul Kumar

September 10, 2020

Acknowledgements

The present handbook is the result of tireless efforts, cooperation, encouragements and blessings of many people. For accomplishment of this book, I have received help from several corners. So, I would like to express my gratitude towards all of them.

First and foremost, I thank almighty God without whose blessings I would not have been here.

I feel great pleasure in expressing my profound sense of gratitude to my revered teachers, Dr. K. K. Gupta, Associate Professor and Dr. A. K. Sharma, Associate Professor, who are presently working at University Department of Zoology, Vinoba Bhave University, Hazaribag, Jharkhand, for their keen interest and guidance during preparation of this handbook.

I owe my most valuable thanks to my parents, Maa and Papa, and sisters, Priyanka and Beauty, witout whose blessings, love and cooperation it would not have been possible to complete this handbook.

Rahul Kumar
September 10, 2020

About The Author

Rahul Kumar is working as Assistant Professor of Zoology at Sheodeni Sao College, Kaler which is a constituent college of Magadh University, Bodh Gaya. He has also worked in many other renowned academic institutions of India like Jawaharlal Nehru University (JNU), New Delhi, National Council of Educational Research and Training (NCERT), New Delhi, Indian Agricultural Research Institute (IARI), New Delhi and All India Institute of Medical Sciences (AIIMS), New Delhi as a research scholar. He has published many scientific research articles. He has worked extensively on the Biology of edible mushrooms. His major areas of research are Molecular Biology, Integrative Taxonomy and Nanobiotechnology.

CHAPTER ONE

PROTEINS

"There is present in plants and animals a substance which ... is without doubt the most important of the known substances in living matter, and without it, life would be impossible on our planet. This material has been named Protein."

-Gerardus Johannes Mulder (1802-1880)

Proteins occupy a central position in the architecture and functioning of living matter. They are intimately connected with all phases of chemical and physical activity, that constitute the life of the cell (White, Handler and Smith, 1964). They are therefore, essential to cell structure and function. Proteins are the essential components of protoplasm, forming the physical basis of life. The proteins with catalytic activity (enzymes) are largely responsible for determining the phenotype or properties of a cell in a particular environment. Thus, the tremendous diversity of living system is essentially due to this organic compound. The total hereditary material of the cell or genotype dictates which type of protein the cell can produce. In fact, the proteins have built into their structure the information that instructs them in "what to do" (catalytic activity), "where to go" in the cell (intracellular organization) and "when and how to perform" (control of function through interaction of proteins with other proteins, small activators or inhibitors). The proteins are therefore referred as body builders.

The term protein (Greek, *proteios* = pre-eminent or first) was first suggested, in 1838, by a Swedish chemist Berzelius to a Dutch chemist Mulder, who referred it to the complex organic nitrogenous substances found in the cells of the living beings. They are most abundant intracellular macro-molecules and constitute over half the dry weight of most organisms. Thus in about 1.5 million species of living organisms, there are probably 1 trillion (10^{12}) different kinds of protein molecules.

Proteins are polymers of amino acids which are interlinked by the peptide bonds. The major constituent elements of proteins are carbon, hydrogen, oxygen and nitrogen. Sulfur is found in minor quantity. In certain complex proteins, other elements like iron, copper, cobalt, zinc, phosphorus, selenium and nickel occur as well.

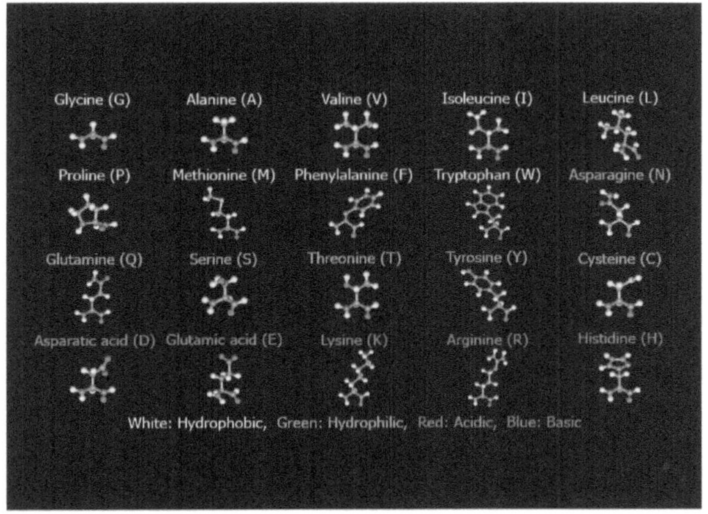

20 Amino Acids

The major elemental composition of proteins in plants and animals presents a great deal of variation. Most animal proteins contain from 0.5 to 2.0 per cent sulfur (Insulin is, however, a notable exception to this in possessing about 3.4% sulfur).

The major elemental composition of proteins in plants and animals presents a great deal of variation (Table-1). Most animal proteins contain from 0.5 to 2.0 per cent sulfur (Insulin is, however, a notable exception to this in possessing about 3.4% sulfur).

Protein	Carbon	Hydrogen	Oxygen	Nitrogen
Green plants	54	7	38	0.003
Mammals	21	10	62	3.0

TABLE-1: Elemental Composition of Plant and Animal Proteins

Proteins perform a great variety of functions. Proteins are very important for growth and repair of the body and are of prime biological importance. Their acute deficiency in the food causes retardation of the physical and mental growth. Deficiency of proteins causes **PEM** (Protein Energy Malnutrition) diseases in infants like **marasmus** and **kwashiorkar.**

CHAPTER TWO

PROTEIN REQUIREMENTS

Protein requirements can be determined by measuring nitrogen balance. The state of protein nutrition can be determined by measuring the dietary intake and output of nitrogenous compounds from the body. Although nucleic acids also contain nitrogen, protein is the major dietary source of nitrogen and measurement of total nitrogen intake gives a good estimate of protein intake (mg N × 6.25 = mg protein, as nitrogen is 16% of most proteins). The output of nitrogen from the body is mainly in urea and smaller quantities of other compounds in urine and undigested protein in feces, and significant amounts may also be lost in sweat and shed skin. The difference between intake and output of nitrogenous compounds is known as nitrogen balance. Three states can be defined: In a healthy adult, nitrogen balance is in equilibrium when intake equals output, and there is no change in the total body content of protein. In a growing child, a pregnant woman, or in recovery from protein loss, the excretion of nitrogenous com- pounds is less than the dietary intake and there is net retention of nitrogen in the body as protein, i.e., positive nitrogen balance. In response to trauma or infection or if the intake of protein is inadequate to meet requirements—there is net loss of protein nitrogen from the body, i.e., negative nitrogen balance. The continual catabolism of tissue proteins creates the requirement for dietary protein even in an adult who is not growing, though some of the amino acids released can be reutilized. Nitrogen balance studies show that the average daily requirement is 0.6 g of protein per kilogram of body weight (the factor 0.75 should be used to allow for individual variation), or approximately 50 g/d. Average intakes of protein in developed countries are about 80–100 g/d, i.e., 14–15% of energy intake. Because growing children are increasing the protein in the body, they have a proportionately greater requirement than adults and should be in positive nitrogen balance.

Not all proteins are nutritionally equivalent. More of some than of others is needed to maintain nitrogen balance because different proteins contain different amounts of the various amino acids. The body's requirement is for specific amino acids in the correct proportions to replace the body proteins. The amino acids can be divided into two groups: essential and nonessential. There are nine essential or indispensable amino acids, which cannot be synthesized in the body: histidine, isoleucine, leucine, lysine, methionine, phenylalanine, threonine, tryptophan, and valine. If one of these is lacking or inadequate, then-regardless of the total intake of protein- it will not be possible to maintain nitrogen balance since there will not be enough of that amino acid for protein synthesis. Two amino acids-cysteine and tyrosine- can be synthesized in the body, but only from essential amino acid precursors (cysteine from methionine and tyrosine from phenylalanine). The dietary intakes of cysteine and tyrosine thus affect the requirements for methionine and phenylalanine. The remaining 11 amino acids in proteins are considered to be nonessential or dispensable, since they can be synthesized as long as there is enough total protein in the diet- i.e., if one of these amino acids is omitted from the diet, nitrogen balance can still be maintained. However, only three amino acids- alanine, aspartate, and glutamate- can be considered to be truly dispensable; they are synthesized from common metabolic intermediates (pyruvate, oxaloacetate, and α-ketoglutarate, respectively). The remaining amino acids are considered as nonessential, but under some circumstances the requirement for them may outstrip the organism's capacity for synthesis.

One of the metabolic reactions to major trauma, such as a burn, a broken limb, or surgery, is an increase in the net catabolism of tissue proteins. As much as 6–7% of the total body protein may be lost over 10 days. Prolonged bed rest results in considerable loss of protein because of atrophy of muscles. Protein is catabolized as normal, but without the stimulus of exercise it is not completely replaced. Lost protein is replaced during convalescence, when there is positive nitrogen balance. A normal diet is adequate to permit this replacement (Table-2).

PROTEIN REQUIREMENTS

Age Group	Age, years	Weight, kg	Height, cm	Protein, g
Infants	0.0-0.5	6	60	kg * 2.2
	0.5-1.0	9	71	Kg * 2
Children	1-3	13	90	23
	4-6	20	112	30
	7-10	28	132	34
Males	11-14	45	157	45
	15-18	66	176	56
	19-22	70	177	56
	23-50	70	178	56
	51+	70	178	56
Females	11-14	46	157	46
	15-18	55	163	46
	19-22	55	163	44
	23-50	55	163	44
	51+	55	163	44
Pregnant				+30
Lactating				+20

Table-2: Daily Dietary Allowances of Proteins Recommended by the Food and Nutrition Board, National Academy of Science-National Research Council, USA (Revised 1980)

MUSHROOMS AS RICH SOURCES OF PROTEINS

Main sources of animal proteins are: fish (16.5%), meat (22%), eggs (11.9%), milk, etc. And main sources of plant proteins are: pulses, soyabean, peas (5.2%), beans, cereals, etc. Soyabean is regarded as the best source of plant proteins. These are traditional sources of proteins.

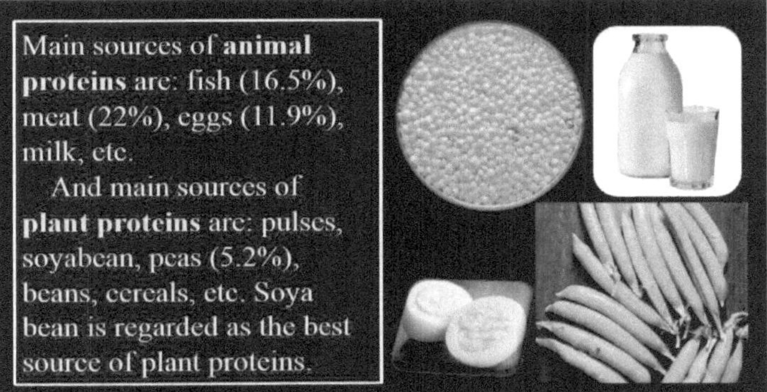

Conventional Sources of Proteins

Mushrooms are higher fungi (macrofungi), belonging to the class Ascomycetes (e.g. *Morchella, Tuber,* etc.) and Basidiomycetes (e.g. *Agaricus, Auricularia, Tremella,* etc.). They are characterized by having heterotrophic mode of nutrition. They may be edible or non-edible. According to Chang and Hayes (1978), edible mushroom refers to both epigeous and hypogeous fruiting bodies of macroscopic fungi that are already commercially cultivated or grown in half culture process or implemented under controlled conditions. Atkins (1983) and Bel (1976) have described following five different groups of edible mushroom. These are:

1. Those which grow on fresh or almost fresh residue, e.g. *Pleurotus* and *Lentius.*
2. Those which grow on slightly composted material, e.g. *Volvariella* and *Coprinus.*
3. Those which grow on well composted material, e.g. *Agaricus.*
4. Those that grow on soil and humus, e.g. *Morchella.*
5. Mycorrizal fungi, e.g. *Boletus* and *Cantharellus.*

Mushrooms are rich in protein and constitute a valuable source of supplementary food. Use of mushrooms can contribute positively in facing the challenge of world-wide food shortage, originating with rapidly expanding human population at the rate of more than 2 lakh per day.

In developed countries, the average consumption of animal protein is about 31 kg per capita per year, whereas it is only 4 kg in India. In India, the plant proteins are more widely used than the animal proteins. Mushrooms are the richest source of vegetable proteins. They contain 21-30% proteins on dry weight basis. Thus the percentage of proteins in mushrooms is much higher than in cereals, pulses, fruits or vegetables. The proteins of mushrooms containall essential amino acids and their quantity is higher than in the egg. There is also a good amount of lysine amino acid in mushrooms (about 550 mg/g).

Generally, mushroom contains 85-90 per cent water of its dry matter. However, amount of water is greatly influenced by relative humidity and temperature during growth and storage.

Besides, mushrooms contain sufficient quantities of mineral elements, such as Ca, Na, P and K. They also contain folic acid and are as such very good source of iron. They contain vitamins B, C, D and K, which are not distorted during ripening, freezing or canning process. On the other hand, they contain very little fats (0.35-0.65% dry wt) and starches (0.02% dry wt). Thus mushrooms make an excellent food for diabetic and heart patients.

Mushroom	*Agaricus bisporus*	*Pleurotus flabellatus*	*Volvariella diplasia*
Moisture	89.50	90.95	90.40
Ash	1.26	0.97	1.10
Protein	3.94	2.78	3.90
Fat	0.16	0.65	0.25
Carbohy-drates	6.28	5.33	5.51
Energy value (cal)	34.4	24.4	29.2

TABLE-3: The Chemical Composition of Three Common Edible Mushrooms

CHAPTER FOUR

STATUS OF MUSHROOM CULTIVATION IN INDIA

Mushrooms have attracted a large number of workers as these have been recognized as plants of great economic importance- as medicine, food, etc. This has resulted into accumulation of abundant literature. Besides work on taxonomy; edible and non- edible nature; genetics and conservation, biochemical analyses have also attracted attention of many workers. Bano (1976), Anderson and Fellers (1942), and Khanna and Gharcha (1981) have contributed to the detail information about food value of mushrooms. Chang (1980), Hussain (2001), Tewari (1986), Nagaratna and Mallesha (2007) and Oei (1996) have contributed to different methodologies of mushroom cultivation with special reference to developing nations. The studies of Fasidi, Ekuere and Usukama (1993); Okhuoya, Isikhuemhen and Evan (1998); Onuoha, Ukaulon and Onuoha (2009); Khan, Kausar and Ali (1981); Krishnamurthy (1981); Kurtzman (1976); Shah, Ashraf and Ishtiaq (2004); and Zardazil (1978) focus upon different aspects of different species and varieties of *Pleurotus*. The most recent work of Somashekhar, Reddy and Vedamurthy (2010) focuses on the methods of spawn inoculation for better yield of mushroom, *Plerotus florida*.

In India, mushroom cultivation started long before a century, as the *Volvariella valvacea* was cultivated on paddy straw. Therefore, this mushroom is also known as the paddy straw mushroom. In 1950s, an attempt was made to cultivate mushroom in Coimbatore (Thomas *et al.*, 1943). In 1962, *Pleurotus flabellatus* (*Dhingri coroyester*) was successfully cultivated in Mysore. Besides many attempts, its cultivation could not be popularized upto the late 1960s. For the first time an attempt was made for artificial cultivation of *A. bisporus* at Solan (Himachal Pradesh) where synthetic compost preparation technology was developed, by using horse dung and wheat straw. Rapid development took place at this centre. Modern Spawn Laboratory and Air Conditioned Cropping rooms were constituted under the guidance of an expert from Food and Agricultural Organizations (FAO).

From 1974, a coordinated scheme was launched at Solan, Bangalore, Ludhiana and New Delhi. FAO deputed its experts for improving the cultivation technology. Dr. W.A. Hayes came to India, who recommended for incorporation of molasses and brewer's grain in the preparation of synthetic compost. This increased the mushroom yield. In 1977, State Department of Horticulture (H.P.) launched a project of Rs. 1.27 crore, under which a Central Mother Unit (CMU) for bulk pasteurization of compost and casing soil was established. CMU supplies about 80 tonnes of pasteurized compost per month to growers in Solan, Shimla and Sirmur districts (Sohi, 1988). During 1966-70 mushroom cultivation was introduced in Kashmir Valley, where by the end of 1975, the number of growers increased to 90. This took up its cultivation as cottage industry in Srinagar and Jammu region.

In 1974, Uttar Pradesh Department of Agriculture (UPDA) started mushroom cultivation on exploratory trial at Vivekanand Parvatiya Krishi Anushandhan (VPKA), Almora. U.P. Govt. also sanctioned a project for mushroom cultivation to the Department of Botany, Kumaun University, Nainital. At Almora Centre, two crops in a year are raised (i.e. in February-April and September-November) in natural conditions. The compost is prepared from agro-wastes i.e. straw of wheat, barley and oat and dehulled corn cobs, grasses, fresh leaves, etc.

Since 1983, a large number of growers started mushroom cultivation during winter around Delhi, Chandigarh and some districts of Haryana (e.g. Sonepat, Rohtak, Karnal) and Punjab (e.g. Ferozpur, Patiala, Ludhiana and Jalandhar). In Bhiwani district of Haryana, mushroom cultivation is gaining much popularity. Under the guidance of specialists of Krishi Gyan Kendra and scientists of Haryana Agriculture University (Hissar) the farmers in villages Tagrana and Bamla have undertaken cultivation of mushrooms. These villages have been declared as mushroom villages.

Since mushrooms have a very short life, it should reach to consumers within a short time or immediately canned. This will lead to proper marketing of mushrooms. Improper care for marketing results in the increase in price. Different technologies for cultivation and processing of mushrooms have been developed at CFTRI (Central Food

Technological Research Institute), Hyderabad, RRL (Regional Research Laboratory), Jammu and NBRI (National Botanical Research Institute), Lucknow. RRL and NBRI are distributing mushroom spawns in rural areas for mass cultivation. CFTRI has developed technique for processing and drying mushrooms.

CHAPTER FIVE

PLEUROTUS FLORIDA: THE OYSTER MUSHROOM

Pleurotus is one of the important mushrooms gaining popularity in recent years. It is found growing naturally on dead organic materials rich in cellulose. Its several species are edible such as *P. sajor-caju, P. sapidus, P. flabellatus, P. ostriatus, P. corticatus, P. florida,* etc. These species can be cultured successfully on various agricultural, domestic, industrial and forestry waste materials. It is very versatile in nature as far as substrate preference and growth are concerned. However, it can be grown on paddy straw, gunny bags, rice husk, copped *Parthenium* stem, etc.

Pleurotus florida is commonly known as White Oyster mushroom due to resemblance of its mature fruiting body with shell of Oyster (a mollusc) and white colour. In India, it is locally known as the **Dhingri mushroom**. It is one of the species of mushrooms widely cultivated at many

KVK (Krishi Vigyan Kendra) centres of Indian Council of Agricultural Research (ICAR) all across India. It is generally grown whole of the year except in the summer season. It can be grown on a variety of substrates. Its cultivation does not require much space. It has comparatively smaller generation time. Its cultivation does not require much financial input.

Scientific Classification of *Pleurotus florida:*

Kingdom – **Fungi**

Phylum – **Basidiomycota**

Class – **Agaricomycetes**

Order – **Agaricales**

Family – **Pleurotaceae**

Genus – ***Pleurotus***

Species – ***florida***

Pleurotus florida **Growing on Paddy Straw**

CHAPTER SIX

CULTIVATION OF PLEUROTUS FLORIDA

The given method of cultivation of *Pleurotus florida* is based on the training provided to the farmers or those interested in mushroom culture at the Mushroom Training Unit and the Mushroom Spawn Unit of Holy Cross- Krishi Vigyan Kendra, Canary Hill, Hazaribagh, Jharkhand.

1. Preparation of Culture Medium

The culture medium contains all the nutrients for microbial growth. Culture media may be of solid or liquid types. Potato-Dextrose-Agar (PDA) is a solid medium specifically suitable for growth and maintenance of common fungi under artificial environmental conditions.

For preparing PDA medium, 50 g of boiled and peeled potatoes are taken. The potatoes are mashed in 100 ml of water and boiled. The solution is filtered with a cheese cloth to obtain potato extract in a beaker. 5 g dextrose is added and the volume of the solution is made upto 250 ml by adding additional 150 ml of water. The pH is measured and adjusted to 7.5. The mixture is warmed in a water bath up to 60°C. 5 g Agar is added and dissolved slowly. The final mixture is boiled till the culture becomes transparent. The culture medium is then autoclaved at 15 lb/inch^2 pressure for 10min. After autoclaving, the medium is brought inside the pre-disinfected laminar flow chamber for media plate preparation.

2. Obtaining Pure Culture

Sterilized and cooled PDA medium is poured into sterile Petri dishes and when solidified they were inoculated by a piece of tissue or spore(s) of mushroom inside the laminar flow chamber. Petri dishes are incubated at suitable temperature (here 20-25°C) for growth of hyphae (Chang and Li, 1982). After one week, fungal growth is found covering the whole surface of mediun in the Petri dish.

3. Preparation of Spawn

Spawn is a fungal growth impregnated with mycelial fragments of mushroom which serves as inoculum for mushroom cultivation. Many substrates are used for spawn making either alone or in combinations. For the selection of substrates to be used in making spawn, care is taken for cost and availability of raw materials and mycelia growth on it as well.

For preparing spawn, wheat grains are used. The wheat grains are boiled in water until they swelled and soaked in water for 5-10min. Water is decanted and 2 percent lime (calcium carbonate) is mixed. Then, grains are transferred into glass tubes. The tubes are plugged with cotton and autoclaved at 121°C for 30min and cooled down to 30-40°C. The grains are inoculated with pure culture of mushroom and incubated at suitable temperature for proper infestation of mycelium for its use as spawn (Chang and Li, 1982). Krishi Vigyan Kendras (KVKs) from all around

India provide spawns to the farmers for free of cost or at a very minimal price for mushroom farming.

4. Substrate Preparation for Cultivation

The mushroom is grown on plant straw. Since paddy straw is easily available and cheap, it is widely used. Paddy straw used should be fresh and well dried. Paddy straw is chopped into 3-5 cm pieces and soaked in fresh water for 8-16 hours. Excess water from straw is drained off by spreading it on filter paper followed by heat treatment. Heat treatment of substrate results in minimizing contamination problem and gives higher and almost constant yields. It can be done by pasteurization. For pasteurization, water is boiled in a wide mouth container such as tub or drum. The wet substrate is filled in side gunny bags. The filled bag is dipped in hot water of 80-85°C for about 10-15 minutes. To avoid floating, it should be pressed with some heavy material or with the help of a wooden piece. After pasteurization, excess hot water is drained off from container.

5. Spawning and Spawn Running

Inoculation by spawn of prepared substrate for mushroom cultivation is known as spawning. When the pasteurized substrate has cooled down to room temperature, it is ready for filling and spawning. At this stage, substrate moisture content is about 70%. Polythene bags (35 x 50 cm) are used for its cultivation. One 500 ml bottle spawn (200- 250g) can be used for 10- 12kg wet straw (3 bags). Spawning can be done in layer spawning or through simple spawning.

In case of layer spawning, substrate is filled in bag, pressed to a depth of 8-10 cm and seeded with a handful of spawn by spreading above it. Similarly, 2nd and 3rd layers of substrate are put and simultaneously after spawning, the bags are closed. In case of simple spawning, pasteurized straw is mixed with 2% spawn and filled in bags. After that it is gently pressed, and the bags are sealed for spawn running (development). Spawned bags are stacked on racks in neat and clean place, in closed position. Temperature at 25-35°C and humidity at 70-85% is maintained by spraying water twice a day on walls and floor. It takes 15- 20 days when bags get fully covered with white mycelium.

Photograph-1   Photograph-2   Photograph-3

Photograph-4   Photograph-5   Photograph-6

DESCRIPTION OF PHOTOGRAPHS

Photograph-1: Mother inoculum containing pure culture of *Pleurotus florida* on wheat grains

Photograph-2: Inoculation on sterile wheat grains to prepare spawns of *Pleurotus florida* in the laminar flow chamber

Photograph-3: Freshly inoculated spawns

Photograph-4: Shelf containing large number of spawns at Mushroom Spawn Unit, Holy-Cross Krishi Vigyan Kendra, Hazaribag

Photograph-5: A worker at Mushroom Spawn Unit, Holy-Cross Krishi Vigyan Kendra, Hazaribaag; showing freshly inoculated spawn (right) and 25 days old spawn (left) for comparison

Photograph-6: Collection of paddy straws for bundle preparation for cultivation of *Pleurotus florida*

6. Cropping and Harvesting

After 20-22 days, when bags are fully impregnated with white mycelium, they are transferred into cropping room and the polythene covers are removed. The open blocks are kept on racks about 20 cm apart with gap of 50-60 cm between two shelves. Mushrooms are grown in a temperature range of 20-33°C. Relative humidity is maintained by spraying water twice a day on the walls and floor of the room. A light spray of water is given on blocks as soon as the small pin heads appeared. Once pinheads are 2-3 cm big a little heavier watering is done on blocks and watering of blocks is stopped to allow them to grow. Mushrooms are plucked before they shed spores to get quality harvest. After 1st flush of harvest, 0.5 to 1 cm outer layer of the block is scrapped. This helps to initiate 2nd flush which appear after 10 days.

After harvesting they are packed in perforated (5-6 small holes) polythene bags to keep them fresh. It loses freshness after about 6 hours, which can be minimized by keeping them in refrigerator.

<u>DESCRIPTION OF PHOTOGRAPHS</u>

PHOTOGRAPH-1: Straw bundles showing different stages of active fungal growth

PHOTOGRAPH-2: Old nutrient-exhausted straw bundles showing minimum fungal growth

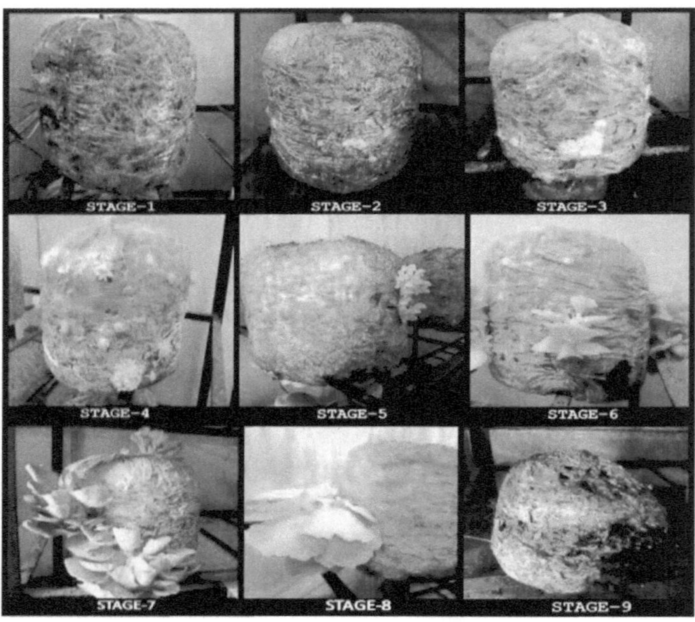

<u>DESCRIPTION OF PHOTOGRAPHS</u>

Different Growth Stages of *Pleurotus florida:*

STAGE-1: Mycelial stage

STAGE-2, 3: Mycelia emerging out of straw bundle to form fruiting bodies

STAGE-4: Early aerial fruiting bodies showing clusters of pin-heads

STAGE-5, 6, 7: Fan like fruiting bodies of different sizes (5<6<7)

STAGE-8: Fully grown fruiting bodies ready for commercial harvesting

STAGE-9: Completely used-up straw bundle (exhausted of nutrients) showing no further growth

Further Readings

Alberts, B., Johnson, A., Lewis, J., Raff, M., Roberts, K., and Walter, P. 2008. *Molecular biology of the cell*, 5th edition. Garland Science, New York

Anderson, E.E. and Fellers, C.R. 1942. Food value of mushrooms (*Agaricus compestris*) Proc. *Amer. Hoot. Sci.* **41**: 301-304

Bendre, A. and Kumar, A. 2005. *A text book of practical botany Vol.1*, 8th edition. Rastogi Publications

Bano, Z. 1976. Nutritive values of Indian mushrooms. *Sci.* 1(2): 473-484

Chang, S.T. 1980. Mushroom production in South East Asia, *Mushroom New lett.* Trop. **1(4)**: 5-10

Curran, B.G., Walker R.J. and Bhatia S.C. 2010. *Bioinformatics*, 1st edition. CBS

Dubey, R.C. 2006. *A textbook of biotechnology*, 1st edition. S.Chand & Company Ltd.

Fasidi, I.O., Ekuere, F. and Usukama,U. 1993. Studies on *Pleurotus tuber-regium* (Fries) singer. Cultivation, proximate composition and mineral content of Sclerotia. *Food Chem.* **48**: 255-258

Hussain, T. 2001. Growing mushroom. *A new Horizon in Agriculture*

Jain, J.L., Jain, S. and Jain, N. 2005. *Fundamentals of biochemistry*, 1st edition. S.Chand & Company Ltd.

Khan, S.M., Kausar, A.G. and Ali, M.A. 1981. Yield performance of different strains of oyster mushrooms (*Pleurotus spp.*) on paddy straw. *Pakistan Mush SciXI Sydney.* **(1)**: 667-75

Khanna, P. and Gharcha, H.S. 1981. Nutritive value of mushroom. *Mushroom Science.* **11**: 561-562

Krishnamurthy, V. 1981. Microbial and chemical studies on the cultivation of oyster mushroom (*Pleurotus sajorcaju*) in paddy straw. *M.Sc. Thesis*, University of Agricultural Sciences, Bangalore.

Kurtzman, R.H. Jr. 1976. Nutrition of *Pleurotus sapidus*- effects of lipids. *Mycologia.* **68**: 268-295

Lakhotia, S.C. 2010. SDS-PAGE for proteins. *ISCB Cell Biology Newsletter.* **30(1)**: 70-74

Murray, Robert K., Granner, Daryl k., Mayes, Peter A. and Rodwell, Victor W. 2003. *Harper's illustrated biochemistry*, 26th edition. Lange Medical Books/McGraw-Hill

Nagaratna, G.K. and Mallesha, B.C. 2007. Use of vermicompost as casing material for cultivation of milky mushroom. *Mushroom Research.* **16(2)**: 81-83

Oei, P. 1996. Mushroom cultivation with special emphasis on appropriate techniques for developing countries. *Tool Publications*, Leiden, Netherlands. pp. 274

Okhuoya, J.A., Isikhuemhen, O.S. and Evan, C.A. 1998. *Pleurotus pulmonarius* (Fries) sing. Sclerotia and sporophore yield during the cultivation on sawdust of different woody plants. *Int. Form Mushroom Sci.* **2**: 41-46

Onuoha, C.I., Ukaulor Uchechi and Onuoha 2009. Cultivation of *Pleurotus pulmonarius* (mushroom) using some agrowaste materials. *Agricultural J.* **4(2)**: 109-112

D. Randive, Sonali, 2012. Cultivation and study of growth of oyster mushroom on different agricultural waste substrate and its nutrient analysis. *Advances in Applied Science Research*, Pelagia Research Library. **3(4)**: 1938-1949

Singh, V., Pande, P.C. and Jain, D.K. 2007. *A text book of botany*, 4th edition. Rastogi Publications

Shah, Z.A., Ashraf, M. and Ishtiaq Ch.M. 2004. Comparative study on cultivation and yield performance of oyster mushroom (*Pleurotus osttreatus*) on different substrates (Wheat straw, Leaves and Saw dust). *Pakistan J. Nutrition.* **(3)**: 158-160

Snustad, D.P. and Simmons, M.J. 2010. *Principles of genetics*, 5th edition. John Wiley & Sons, Inc.

Somashekhar, R., Rakesh Reddy, R. and Vedamurthy A.B. 2010. Cultivation of oyster mushroom (*Pleurotus florida*) on paddy straw by delayed spawn inoculation. *The Bioscan.* **5(1)**: 167-168

Stansfield, William D., Colome, Jaime S. and Cano, Raul J. 2004. *Schaum's outlines of theory and problems of molecular and cell biology*, 1st edition. Tata McGraw-Hill Publishing Company Limited

Tewari, R.P. 1986. Mushroom cultivation. *Extension Bulletin.* Indian Institute of Horticulture Research. Bangalore. India. **8**: 36

Verma, Kesherwani, Sharma, Sawarkar and Singh. 1987. Mineral content of edible mushrooms. *Ind. Journal. Nutr. Dietet.* **24**: 241-245

Wilson, K. and Walker, J. 2000. *Practical biochemistry-principles and techniques*, 5th edition. Cambridge University Press

Zadrazil, F. 1978. Cultivation of *Pleurotus*. In S.T. Chang and W.A. Hayes (Ed). *The biology and cultivation of edible mushroom. Academic Press.* New York. 521-557

The Oyester mushroom is one of the most delicious mushrooms. Their flavour and texture are amazing.